SEEK
HIM
FIRST

How to Hear From God, Walk in His Will, and Change Your World

Jennifer Hayes Yates

Author photo by Genesis Shalom Harrington

Edited by Josiah Lee Yates

Formatted by Jen Henderson at Wild Words Formatting.

TABLE OF CONTENTS

SEEK HIM FIRST—
INTRODUCTION

> **"Look to the LORD and his strength;**
> **seek his face always"**
> **(1 Chronicles 16:11).**

It's been said there are those who observe things happen, and there are those who make things happen. There are those who watch the pot, and there are those who stir the pot. There are those who ride the waves and those who make waves.

It's the wave-makers who change the world.

We all have choices to make every day, yet many of us struggle to know if we are doing the right thing. Are we really hearing from God and walking in His will? We want to be obedient to Christ, but we struggle with relationships, finances, a job we don't like, a child with special needs, health issues, aging parents, and the list goes on.

Jesus forewarned us of these realities.

1

"In this world you will have trouble. But take heart! I have overcome the world" (John 16:33).

We are called to take up our cross and follow Him, but what do we do when that path gets rough and we're unsure of the next steps? How do we get past our struggles to actually make a difference for the kingdom of God?

". . . and anyone who does not take his cross and follow me is not worthy of me. Whoever finds his life will lose it, and whoever loses his life for my sake will find it" (Matthew 10:38-39).

That's exactly where I found myself just a few years after I gave my life to Jesus.

I became a believer during my sophomore year in college, but a new job, a wedding, and a couple of children later, real life hit me like a Mack truck. I was struggling—unhappy in my marriage, impatient with my children, and facing temptations that threatened to run me over. Have you been there?

I really needed to hear from God and know how to walk in His will for my life. I still had a desire in my heart to follow Him and make a difference in the world, but I didn't know how to get the Word I heard at church or I read in my Bible to flesh out in my life.

Then something happened that turned my world around. I made a decision that changed everything for me. I resolved to seek Him first, every day, no matter what.

"But seek first his kingdom and his righteousness, and all these things will be given to you as well" (Matthew 6:33).

I know that sounds a little too simple—but I promise that one decision made all the difference. I want to show you in this book how I did that.

The truth is we need direction for every decision—where to go to college, whom to marry, where to go to church, which job to take, what ministries to be involved in, how to handle our finances, how to handle broken relationships, and so many other things.

Seek Him First has been written to show you exactly how you can seek God and find the direction you need for the journey. This book is for those who know God has a plan for their lives, but don't know how to make it a reality from day to day.

In the pages of this book, I will show you how I learned to spend time with God every day. If you follow these steps, you will be able to commit (and stay committed) to a daily quiet time that will stir up a hunger inside of you for more of God.

You will begin to know when He is speaking to you and follow His plan for your life. And you will be so filled with excitement and zeal when you begin to hear God's voice, that you will no longer be satisfied with just sitting in a pew.

You will have a desire to be on mission with the God of the universe, and that, my friend, will change your world.

I don't want you to miss out on all that God has in store for you. He has great plans for your life—bigger and better than you could ever think or imagine—but you will miss His will for you if you don't learn how to seek Him first.

"Now to him who is able to do immeasurably more than all we ask or imagine, according to his power that is at work within us, to him be glory in the church and in Christ Jesus throughout all generations, for ever and ever! Amen." (Ephesians 3:20-21).

These steps have been proven in my own life and in the lives of many others I know who have learned how to seek the Lord. You don't have to stumble through life never sure of what you're supposed to be doing or how to get through your next trial.

You can learn how to hear God's voice for yourself. So what are you waiting for? Turn the page and discover the reality of seeking Him first.

SECTION 1

HOW TO HEAR FROM GOD

CHAPTER 1

SPEND TIME WITH
GOD EVERY DAY

> "To fall in love with God is the
> greatest romance; to seek him,
> the greatest adventure; to find him,
> the greatest human achievement."
> —St. Augustine

Okay, I know what you're thinking. Duh.

Of course, if we want to hear from God, we need to spend time with Him every day. But just because we know we should do something, doesn't mean we know *how* to do it or that we actually *do* it! I know I need to exercise, but I don't always know what to do or how to get started.

Sound familiar? That's where I was fifteen years ago in my spiritual life. When I became a Christian, I began to read my Bible and pray every day, but soon life got in the way. Once I got married and had children, days would go by without my doing more than whispering a prayer on the way to work.

I would show up at church on Sunday and feel guilty because I knew I hadn't really spent time with the Lord as I should have. Then the temptations would come, and I would be too weak to resist. Pretty soon, I was making excuses for the sin in my life, and I was nowhere near where I should have been in my relationship with the Lord.

I began to grow cold in my relationship with God, and everyone around me suffered for it. The truth is that without daily time with Jesus, not only will we stop growing, but we will also begin drying up spiritually. We will start to lose our spiritual fervor and make excuses for sin in our lives.

Decisions will be harder, life will seem tougher, and everything will become a struggle. I'm not saying every trial and struggle is a result of not seeking the Lord. Certainly we face trials, just as Jesus said we would because we live in a fallen world. But our attitude and perspective is different when we are not following closely to Jesus.

It was at a time just like that one that I decided I had nothing left to lose. My marriage was in chaos, my heart was not right, and my life lacked the joy and peace that I knew I should have in the Lord. I cried out to the Lord, and He answered me.

"In my distress I called to the LORD; I cried to my God for help. From his temple he heard my voice; my cry came before him, into his ears" (Psalm 18:6).

I began to read devotions and books that touched my heart and inspired me to once again spend quality time with the Lord as I once had.

"Yet I hold this against you: You have forsaken your first love. Remember the height from which you have fallen! Repent and do the things you did at first" (Revelation 2:4-5a).

I was so desperate for a change in my life, that I decided I would make a commitment to seek Him first every single day—no excuses.

My life was radically changed.

See, I thought all my problems were because of other people in my life, but God began to show me things I needed to change. It wasn't easy, but day by day I began to grow and mature in my walk with the Lord. My marriage relationship improved, because I took responsibility for the things that I could change, instead of waiting for my husband to change. I also began to develop more peace and patience with my children.

Then as I grew, the Lord began to fill my heart with a passion and desire for more of Him, for making disciples, for worship and the Word, and to be on mission with Him.

I realized that there was more to salvation than getting a ticket to heaven—God desired to radically change my life from the inside out. That's His desire for each of us. We can have as much of the life of God in us as we are willing to surrender of ourselves. We can have as much of the life of God in us as we are willing to let Him have His way.

"Therefore, if anyone is in Christ, he is a new creation; the old has gone, the new come!" (2 Corinthians 5:17).

My life hasn't been perfect since that life-changing decision to seek Him first, but my heart has been forever changed as I have fallen in love with the King of kings.

I began to notice that when my friends had problems, my advice to them would always be the same: set aside time every day to seek God.

No matter what our issues in life—physical, emotional, financial, relational, social, mental, or spiritual—we can find the direction and answers we need by seeking God.

"The lions may grow weak and hungry, but those who seek the Lord lack no good thing" (Psalm 34:10).

He Wants Us to Know Him

From creation to the cross, God's plan for mankind has always been for us to know Him. God desires a relationship with each of us—not just adherence to a religious belief. We do have to believe in Him, but the Word says even the demons believe and they shudder. Simply believing in Him is not the same as truly getting to know Him.

"You believe that there is one God. Good! Even the demons believe that—and shudder" (James 2:19).

Lots of people believe in God, but they don't have a personal relationship with Him. Many actually take the step of becoming a "Christian," but they never get past the outward religious steps that seem to characterize Christians—you know, go to church, say your prayers, get a Christian t-shirt, stop cussing, and pay your tithe.

Those things are all great—but they don't necessarily reflect a change of heart. God wants our hearts.

"For where your treasure is, there your heart will be also" (Matthew 6:21).

"Jesus replied: 'Love the Lord your God with all your heart and with all your soul and with all your mind'" (Matthew 22:37).

God created the world and made us in His image. Sin came into the world through Adam and Eve, but God was always making a way to cover our sin and draw our hearts back to Him. From the Ten Commandments given to show us our sin to the tabernacle system of worship instituted to make atonement for our sin to the prophets sent to warn man of the consequence of sin, God's desire was relationship with His people.

The ultimate demonstration of that desire was in sending His Son.

"But God demonstrates his own love for us in this: while we were still sinners, Christ died for us" (Romans 5:8).

God sent Jesus into the world to die for our sins so that we could know Him. He is holy. We are not. Only the blood of Christ could make a way for us to be with God forever. That same blood and faith in Him is what also draws us into a right relationship with Him now.

"I am the good shepherd; I know my sheep and my sheep know me—just as the Father knows me and I know the Father—and I lay down my life for the sheep" (John 10:14-15).

"My sheep listen to my voice; I know them, and they follow me" (John 10:27).

"Now this is eternal life: that they may know you, the only true God, and Jesus Christ, whom you have sent" (John 17:3).

Salvation is not just about getting a ticket punched for heaven—it's about knowing the God who created us and living in an intimate relationship with Him while we are here on earth.

Let's say you are lost and your life is in shambles. You're deep in sin. Then you make a decision that you are going to turn over a new leaf. You decide to leave behind your old friends, quit cussing, lying, and drinking, and go to church.

Awesome, right?

So now your life is better because you have a new set of friends at church, you have guidelines to live by, and you finally have some stability in your life rather than chaos.

Honestly, any religion can give you that—even joining a gang can give you a new group of friends and a new set of rules to live by.

But what happens when the new friends fail you, you can't keep the rules, and God doesn't fix all your problems? You see, that change is just a religious one, and those changes will satisfy for a little while. The enemy's deception is to keep you satisfied with religion until you fall for the lie that there is nothing else.

This peace doesn't last, because it's not real peace. The only real peace is peace with God. That peace doesn't come through our decision to go to church or follow the Bible or change our ways. We can't change ourselves anyway. Jesus is the only One who can cleanse us from sin.

"Wash away all my iniquity and cleanse me from my sin" (Psalm 51:2).

"Cleanse me with hyssop, and I will be clean; wash me and I will be whiter than snow" (Psalm 51:7).

"Create in me a pure heart, O God, and renew a steadfast spirit within me" (Psalm 51:10).

"But you were washed, you were sanctified, you were justified in the name of the Lord Jesus Christ and by the Spirit of our God" (1 Corinthians 6:11).

Real peace is only found in a relationship with Him. Real peace is the result of surrendering our lives to God and allowing Him to change us from the inside out. We will want to go to church. We will leave behind the places that drew us into sin. We will make new friends in Christ. We will want to read the Bible and do God's will.

None of that will come as a result of our decision to do anything except surrender to Jesus.

I know, because that's what happened in my life. I made a decision that I wanted to become a Christian, but I was trying to "do all the right things" in my own strength, without really seeking to know God.

Having a relationship with God is more than just knowing Him. It is deeper than that. God created us for spiritual intimacy with Him. That's why Christians are called the Bride of Christ. God has pursued us and drawn us to Him. He desires us. He wants to know us, and He wants us to know Him—intimately.

"But whatever was to my profit I now consider loss for the sake of Christ. What is more, I consider everything a loss compared to the surpassing greatness of knowing Christ Jesus my Lord, for whose sake I have lost all things. I consider them rubbish, that I may gain Christ" (Philippians 3:7-8).

Marriage is supposed to be a reflection of our relationship with the Lord. In a good marriage, two people give each other their most important resource: time.

"'For this reason a man will leave his father and mother and be united to his wife, and the two will become one flesh.' This is a profound mystery—but I am talking about Christ and the church" (Ephesians 5:31-32).

Shift Your Mindset

So maybe you are like I was—you know you need more of God in your life, you need to hear His voice and seek His direction. If that is the case, then you need to make a shift in your mindset. Instead of thinking of God as One who will reveal your future like a fortune-teller, think of Him as One who desires a relationship with you. Out of that relationship will come the direction that you need for your life.

Once we begin to see God as One who desires relationship with us, then we will understand that we need to plan, prepare, and position ourselves for time with Him.

For instance, if we want to have a good marriage, we have to date our spouse. We need to plan for times alone with him. We prepare by making dinner reservations or hiring a babysitter. We have to position ourselves to spend time with our spouse by sitting down in a restaurant or movie theater or going on a walk with him. We have to be intentional about dating our spouse. Otherwise, life will get in the way.

We also need to plan for time with the Lord, come to that time prepared, and position ourselves to hear His voice. Before we go to the next chapter, let's think about a few questions:

Do you struggle to know God's direction for your life?

Do you spend quality time with the Lord each day?

What normally gets in the way of your seeking God each day?

In the next chapter, we are going to look at what consistent, quality time with God every day looks like. But you don't have to wait until you know everything. Just make that mindset shift and decide that you will seek God first, starting right now.

Take a few minutes, right now, and talk to God.

CHAPTER 2

PLAN, PREPARE, AND POSITION YOURSELF

> **"Continue seeking God with seriousness. Unless he wanted you, you would not be wanting him."**
> **—C.S. Lewis**

When I decided to seek God first every day, I struggled with the time. My children were little, and I was a full-time teacher. In order to have actual quiet time to spend with God without the distractions and responsibilities of family pulling at me, I had to make a decision to get up earlier than everyone else.

Plan

I'm not a morning person—especially back then. All I ever wanted to do was sleep. I really struggled with the whole getting-up-early-decision. I tried for a while to have my quiet time in the evenings. I figured after everyone went to bed and it was quiet, I would be able to focus on the Lord without distractions.

But I was too tired! By then I had worked all day, cooked supper, cleaned house, done laundry, made lunches, given baths, and helped with homework. I would be too drained to really focus on the Word or hear anything from God. I know some of you may be more alert and do enjoy your quiet time at night, but nighttime devotions just didn't work for me.

I tried coming in right after school while the kids were doing homework and Kenneth, my husband, wasn't home yet. But there were always too many distractions, such as chores and laundry that I knew needed to be done.

I finally realized that I would have to set aside time early, and that I would not be at peace in my life until I did. I set my alarm for thirty minutes earlier than usual. I programmed my coffee pot as well, so I could get started as soon as possible.

Prepare

I had found that when I didn't prepare for my quiet time, my mind would wander. I would sit there drinking coffee, thinking about a million other things until I had run out of time. So, I decided to begin preparing for my time with the Lord.

I bought a daily devotional book, a journal, and a set of pens. I got some sticky notes so that if an errant thought came, I could jot it down and go back to my quiet time. I gathered all my materials along with my study Bible, and I put them all together in a basket beside my chair in the living room. I made sure there was a lamp beside the chair because I knew it would still be dark outside.

I got up the next morning, washed my face, brushed my teeth, and got my coffee. I sat down in that chair and opened my devotion, and God began to speak to me.

As I read the devotion, I looked up the Scripture that went with it. I opened my journal, wrote down the date, and then copied that verse. Then I journaled back to God what I felt He was saying to me through that verse and that devotion.

Next, I wrote Praise—Psalm 1. The Lord led me to start my prayer time with praise. What better way to praise Him than through the Psalms? So I read Psalm 1, and I thought about how I could apply that Scripture to my own life. I journaled those thoughts and prayers to God.

Next, I wrote Confession. I asked God to show me every single thing in my heart, my mind, my attitude, my motives, and my mouth that was not right with Him. As I began to write, the tears began to flow and I repented of all the sin I had allowed to take hold in my life.

Suddenly, the clock showed I had to get moving, and I hadn't even finished with my plan! I went about my business that day, but I knew God was doing a work in my life, cleansing me and turning my heart back to Him. I realized He had much more to say to me.

That day went better than many days had for a long time, and I realized that real, quality time in His presence was what I had lacked in my relationship with God. The spiritual dryness, the emptiness—it had nothing to do with God or Kenneth or anybody else and everything to do with me.

Position Yourself

That night as I set my clock, I realized I wanted more time with God. I wasn't any more tired that day than I had been on any other day, so why not? So I set my clock one hour earlier than usual. I learned that if I would make the effort to position myself to hear from God by getting up early and seeking Him first, He would speak.

I got up the next morning and started with the same process as the day before: I put down the date, read the devotion, and wrote down the Scripture and what I felt God was saying to me. I continued with Praise—Psalm 2, Confession, and this time, I kept going even further! I began to write out my prayer requests, asking God to work in my heart, drawing me closer to Him, and I prayed the same for my family and those I love. I prayed to be a better wife, mother, and teacher. I prayed for my students and that God would lead me throughout the day.

Again, my time was over much too quickly, but I was coming alive! I was beginning to feel God's presence in my life again. And I wanted more.

As I continued this process, day after day, I added Thanks as my next category, and I would take time every day to write out all the things I was thankful for. The list would be different every day as God would reveal all the answered prayers, protection, and provision in my life. I became a more grateful person as a result.

Over time, I added Bible reading in the New Testament. I started with Matthew. I would read a little each day until I felt God had spoken through those verses and I would write it down. Over several years, I eventually read all of the New Testament and started back at Genesis and read all the way through the Old Testament. When I got to things I didn't understand, I would read the study notes in my Bible.

Last, I added a section to my quiet time that I called Listen. I would just sit quietly before the Lord and listen for His still, small voice. After many months of reading His Word, I knew His voice and I could discern what agreed with His Word. This section has become my favorite part of my quiet time.

Over the years, the process has changed from time to time. I have added and changed some of the things I do. Sometimes I play worship music and sing. One day I wrote a poem in my quiet time. Spending time with the Lord is similar to when you are dating and you think of new things to do with your mate: you may bring him a gift, bake a special dessert, write him a poem, or leave him a love note.

We think about how to express our love to our husbands or children, and we can do the same with the Lord. Be creative and enjoy your time with Him. I think He delights in that.

I now enjoy doing Bible studies and have added an extra hour in the mornings to do Bible study. If I need to start getting ready for work at 6:30, I get up at 4:30.

Now listen to my heart: I'm not saying everybody needs to get up at 4:30 to be a good Christian. I'm not even saying that everybody needs to spend two hours with the Lord. What I want you to take away from my story is this: the more time I spend with Him, the more I want. I consider giving God two of the twenty-four hours He has given me each day to be small compared to all He has done for me.

God is so good! He loves us, desires us, pursues us, and longs to spend time with us. He wants us to know Him and He wants to know us intimately. We can have just as much of Him in our lives as we want.

"And I pray that you, being rooted and established in love, may have power together with all the saints, to grasp how wide and long and high and deep is the love of Christ, and to know this love that surpasses knowledge—that you may be filled to the measure of all the fullness of God" (Ephesians 3:17b-19).

My goal is to encourage you to seek Him for yourself and find the joy, peace, and excitement that come from seeking His face and His heart.

"And without faith it is impossible to please God, because anyone who comes to him must believe that he exists and that he rewards those who earnestly seek him" (Hebrews 11:6).

I know many people who have their quiet time and Bible study at night. I know people who do quiet time in the morning and Bible study at night.

Your personality will determine what is best for you.

I'm not a morning person, but I love mornings! In other words, I would rather sleep, and I enjoy the days that I get to sleep later. But once I am up and awake, I love the morning time itself. I love that quietness and stillness when the earth is still asleep. I love to watch the light break over the horizon and hear the birds as they bring forth the dawn.

"In the morning, O LORD, you hear my voice; in the morning I lay my requests before you and wait in expectation" (Psalm 5:3).

"Satisfy us in the morning with your unfailing love, that we may sing for joy and be glad all our days" (Psalm 90:14).

"Let the morning bring me word of your unfailing love, for I have put my trust in you. Show me the way I should go, for to you I lift up my soul" (Psalm 143:8).

"He wakens me morning by morning, wakens my ear to listen like one being taught" (Isaiah 50:4b).

Morning isn't for everyone, but I do encourage you to try it, even if you aren't a morning person. You might be surprised that God will give you a love for that time as He has for me.

The important thing is to pick a time that works for you consistently, day in and day out. Make a commitment to seek God every day.

I titled this book *Seek Him First* because of Matthew 6:33:

"But seek first his kingdom and his righteousness, and all these things will be given to you as well."

I believe that our time is kind of like our money—we should give God the firstfruits of it. In the Old Testament, the Israelites were commanded to bring the firstfruits of their crops to the Lord as an offering.

"Bring the best of the firstfruits of your soil to the house of the LORD your God" (Exodus 23:19).

The firstfruits offering was a way the Israelites acknowledged that everything came from God, and now they were giving back to Him out of their gratitude for His provision. When we bring our tithe to the Lord, I believe we should set aside what we are going to give first, and budget everything else around that.

The same applies to our time.

In other words, we need to give Him the best, not what's left, or just whatever we can fit in. But let me give you a different perspective if you just aren't the type to have your quiet time in the morning.

First fruits are the *best* of whatever we have to offer. What is your best time—when you are the most energized, focused, creative, and productive? If it's the middle of the day, make your quiet time at lunch. If it's late at night, then go for it.

So when I say "Seek Him first," my point is that time with Him needs to be our number one priority that nothing can keep us from. In other words, no matter when you plan for your quiet time, family, friends, vacation, television, appointments, careers, nothing, nothing, nothing, will keep you from that commitment.

Once I made that decision to seek God in my life, nothing has ever kept me from doing it. I have met with God every single day for over fifteen years. I have been through hospitalization, deaths in my family, migraines, and early morning trips, but nothing has ever stopped me from having my quiet time every single day since those early days.

You know why?

I am addicted to the presence of God in my life. I know that I can't make it without Him. I am desperate for His voice and His direction in my life. I know that He will never leave me, but I have experienced what it's like to walk away from Him and do things my own way. It doesn't go well, and I don't ever intend to go back to life without Him.

"We must pay more careful attention, therefore, to what we have heard, so that we do not drift away" (Hebrews 2:1).

In the next chapter, we are going to look at how spending time with God teaches us to recognize His voice, but before we go, think about these questions.

What are the distractions or temptations you face in spending time with God every day?

What are some steps you could take to overcome those?

How could you plan, prepare, and position yourself to hear from God?

Take a few minutes and write down what your plan would look like and how you can prepare for a new quiet time with the Lord.

Download your quiet time guide here to help you get started: https://www.subscribepage.com/yourquiettimeguide

CHAPTER 3

LEARN TO RECOGNIZE GOD'S VOICE

> **"A Bible that's falling apart usually belongs to someone who isn't."**
> **—Charles H. Spurgeon**

I have been married for twenty-five years. I know my husband pretty well. I know a lot about his childhood, even though we didn't know each other then. I know his family (and love them!). I know his favorite color, his favorite foods, what he likes to watch on TV. I know what makes him laugh and what makes him cry.

Even though I know a lot, I still don't know everything about him. For instance, Kenneth grew up playing baseball, all the way from Little League to the state championship in high school. He loves sports, teaches physical education, and is the assistant athletic director for our school district.

I knew that when I married him, and I have learned to enjoy watching many sports with him. But he is not the hunter/fisher type of sportsman. In fact, he doesn't own a single piece of camouflage. So imagine my surprise a couple years ago when I heard him talking to someone at church about the time he went hunting with a friend.

Wait a minute! You mean you actually put on camouflage and went in the woods with a gun? I laughed until my side hurt.

What a thrill that after twenty-five years of marriage there are still new things to discover about my husband and new ways to know him! I love Kenneth more now than I did when we first got married because I know him better. I know more about his character and his love for me. I trust him more because we have been through more together.

That's how our relationship is with God. The more time we spend with Him, the more we will learn about Him, and there are always new things to discover about God. His Word never grows old.

If we want to be able to grow in the Lord and hear His voice, we will have to know His character as revealed to us in His Word. We will know Him, love Him, and trust Him more as we seek Him more. When we face trials in life, our feet must be firmly planted on our faith—not just belief in God but faith in Who He is.

There are many ways to get to know God, but we will know Him best in the one-on-one time that we spend with Him. So how do we learn more of who God is through His Word?

The primary way is through Bible study. I mentioned in the last chapter that after several years of doing daily quiet time, which was mostly devotional in nature, I began to add Bible study to my daily time. That's not to say that I had not studied the Bible prior to that time, but it wasn't something I did every day in my quiet time.

Once I began to spend time in actual Bible study during my quiet time, my understanding of God and His ways grew tremendously. I want to share with you a few methods for Bible study that I enjoy. Most of these I learned from Rick Warren's book, *Bible Study Methods*[1].

First of all, one important aspect of Bible study is application. If we study the Bible for purely academic insight, we may miss out on important application principles. We need a balanced approach to studying for both understanding and application.

Second, quality is better than quantity. Reading through the Bible in a year is great, but only if we are able to retain and apply what we are reading. I have always found that pace to be too fast for me to absorb, so don't feel the pressure of reading a lot at one time. Sometimes one verse gives me food to chew on for days.

Here are a few different methods for studying the Bible. You can try all of them, but I have a couple that are my go-to methods.

Devotional study

Devotional study entails reading a passage of Scripture and asking God to show you how you can apply it to your life. This method is what I used when I first went through the whole Bible over a period of several years. I usually free-write about the passage as the Lord leads me, meaning that I journal my thoughts in response to God's Word. I will sometimes use the cross-references listed, which shows you other verses in the Bible on similar topics or themes. It's a prayerful, meditative way to study the Bible that doesn't require any additional resources.

Word study

This is my second favorite way to study. In the word study method, you can take one word and study the meaning of the word, what it means in its Greek or Hebrew original language, and all of its uses in the Bible. This method requires a Greek and Hebrew concordance or an app, such as *Blue Letter Bible*.

For instance, if you wanted to study the word *worship*, you could look up the meaning of the word in an English dictionary, the original Hebrew and Greek using an exhaustive concordance, and all of the verses containing that word in the Bible. This information can be found in a concordance, such as the *NIV Exhaustive Bible Concordance*.[2]

You could then read those verses in their context to get a better understanding of the use of the word. When you finish (which could take you several days), you would have a better understanding of the word *worship* and how it applies to your life.

Verse study

In a verse study, you write out the verse, study its context, background, and any important words. This method is great for studying God's promises and how they apply to our lives. You can read the cross-references and the study notes in a study Bible and focus on each word in the verse, one at a time.

Memorization is a great tool during verse study, because it allows you to pull that verse from your heart when you need it. Memorizing a verse also helps you to focus on one word at a time.

Topical study

One of my favorite methods is topical study. Let's say you wanted to study the role of women in the Bible. You could use a concordance to look for every passage with the word woman or women. You could also look for the names of famous women in the Bible. Women like Sarah, Hannah, Deborah, Esther, Ruth, and Mary are good ones to start. A Bible handbook would be useful for this study. I like to use the *Nelson's Compact Bible Handbook*[3].

In this method, you want to, again, look for application. What can you learn from their lives? What can their stories teach you about God and His work in your life?

Thematic study

This method uses the same process as a topical study, but follows a particular theme in the Bible, such as *grace*. Look for uses of the word *grace* and explore the context in which it is used. What are some promises involving the word *grace*? What are some warnings? What is God speaking to your heart as you study this word?

Biographical study

I have only done this method as part of Bible studies I purchased, such as Beth Moore's *David[4]*. This method studies the life of one individual in the Bible, researches their background, culture, and character qualities. What can you learn from this person's life, both the positive and the negative aspects?

Chapter or Book Study

This is a big-picture kind of study where you look at the overall background, culture, geography, time period, history, writer, and major theme of a chapter or book of the Bible. Understanding the context of a particular book or even chapter can give you a much deeper understanding of the scriptural content.

Know His Word—Know His Voice

As you can see, there are so many ways to study God's Word—these are just a few. Remember the goal is to learn more about God and His character and how we can apply His Word to our lives.

One of my favorite studies is to study the Gospels and how Jesus interacted with those around Him. It takes a long time, but it's probably one of the most valuable studies you can ever do. You can also study the book of Acts or the life of Paul. These are all great studies that will give you so much insight into the heart of God.

Here's my point: if we want to hear from God and know His will for our lives, we have to know HIM. The only way to know Him is to study His Word.

So many Christians go through life never making an impact for the Kingdom of God because they're just pew-warmers. They never pick up their Bibles from Sunday to Sunday. They never feed themselves; they just show up on Sunday morning and wait for someone else to feed them.

When life hits them hard, they don't know how to handle it. They are desperate for God to get them out of a bad situation. I don't want that for you. Jesus calls us to follow Him and be His disciples. A disciple is a learner or fully-devoted follower.

If we want to hear from God and follow His direction in life, then we need to cultivate an ear that hears His voice. That listening ear will be tuned to the voice of God because time in His Word makes us familiar with what He sounds like.

I can hear Kenneth's voice above any crowd because my ear is tuned to his voice. If we never talked and I never spent time with him, I wouldn't know his voice or be able to recognize his voice in a crowd.

The world is speaking loud and clear. There are many voices vying for our attention and intent on leading us the wrong way. No wonder so many Christians are confused about what is true and what they believe.

But you don't have to be. Spend time with God in His Word and ask for a sanctified ear—one that is set apart to the voice of God. He will speak if we will be still and listen.

"My sheep listen to my voice; I know them, and they follow me" (John 10:27).

"She had a sister called Mary, who sat at the Lord's feet listening to what he said" (Luke 10:39).

". . . let the wise listen and add to their learning, and let the discerning get guidance" (Proverbs 1:5).

As we come to the end of this chapter, take a few minutes to think about these questions.

Do you know when you hear God's voice?

Are you studying the Bible daily?

What's the last thing you heard the Lord say to you?

Which type of Bible study method interests you the most right now?

Before you move into the next chapter, get out your Bible and turn to Psalm 1. Do a devotional study of this short Psalm just to whet your appetite for Bible study. Read the passage slowly and prayerfully, asking God to speak to you through His Word. Then write down what He shows you.

That's you hearing from God, my friend.

SECTION 2

HOW TO WALK
IN GOD'S WILL

CHAPTER 4

STOP EATING
THE WRONG FOOD

> "When your will is God's will,
> you will have your will."
> —Charles H. Spurgeon

In 2005, Kenneth and I went on a mission trip to Guatemala. I had never before witnessed that level of hunger. To see people stand in line for hours to get a small plate of rice, beans, and a tortilla was startling to me.

Because we live in America, most of us don't experience hunger on the level of those in third world countries who don't know what a full belly feels like. But we do experience hunger on some level.

Have you ever been super hungry but didn't have anything really *good* to eat, so you just ate what you could find? It filled you up for the moment, but it didn't really satisfy. Chances are, within an hour or so, you still felt hungry.

We do the same thing spiritually. We feed on things that don't satisfy, and then we're still hungry for something. The problem is we don't know what.

"Jesus answered, 'I tell you the truth, you are looking for me, not because you saw miraculous signs but because you ate the loaves and had your fill. Do not work for food that spoils, but for food that endures to eternal life, which the Son of Man will give you'" (John 6:26-27a).

"Then Jesus declared, 'I am the bread of life. He who comes to me will never go hungry, and he who believes in me will never be thirsty'" (John 6:35).

Jesus said not to work for food that spoils. In other words, we can feed on the wrong things.

Many times we struggle to walk in God's will because we're feeding ourselves the wrong food. Let's look at how we seek to satisfy ourselves with the things that leave us unfulfilled and unsatisfied.

Body, Soul, and Spirit

A helpful framework for understanding the way we function is to think of man as a three-part being: We live in a body, we have a soul, and we are a spirit.

"May God himself, the God of peace, sanctify you through and through. May your whole spirit, soul, and body be kept blameless at the coming of our Lord Jesus Christ" (1 Thess. 5:23).

The Greek word for *body* is *soma* meaning "flesh."[5] This includes our senses and the part of us that relates to our environment.

The Greek for *spirit* is *pneuma* or "breath of God."[6] This is the part of us that relates to God and discerns the spiritual things of life.

The Greek for *soul* is *psuche* meaning "life."[7] This is the part of us that relates to others, such as our personality. The soul is made of three parts: the mind, will, and emotions.

Let's look at the relationship between the body, soul, and spirit.

The body contains our flesh that wants to be satisfied, whether it's with food, sex, or sleep. The flesh is how our body perceives information. If something looks good, sounds good, or feels good, we perceive it as something we want.

Our soul is the mind, will, and emotions. It's with our soul that we process information. Our mind processes the information perceived by the flesh, our emotions decide how we feel about it, and our will makes the decision to partake of it.

As Christians, we are new creations, filled with the Holy Spirit. But we still have a sinful, human nature that seeks to be comforted with unholy things. If we want to hear from God and walk in His will, we have to learn how to stop feeding our flesh whatever it wants. The flesh seeks the things contrary to God's Spirit.

"For the flesh desires what is contrary to the Spirit, and the Spirit what is contrary to the flesh. They are in conflict with each other" (Galatians 5:17).

But I've found that whichever we feed grows, and what we starve dies.

So, let's look at how to starve the flesh.

The Sin Nature

Sinful desires will continue to wage war against our soul—mind, will, and emotions. The Greek word for *abstain* is *apecho* which means "to be distant, avoid, a way off, about seven miles; to have one thing by separating oneself from something else."[8]

Don't you love that??

When I first studied this passage, I was so intrigued with the Greek meaning of the word *abstain*. We are taught the harsh side of this word: Abstain from all sin! But we rarely hear the second part of this definition: "to have one thing by separating oneself from something else."

In other words, we aren't just trying to give up sin in our own power and just for the sake of it. God is holy, and He does call us out of a sinful lifestyle, but He also calls us to something better. He fills us Himself! We separate ourselves from sin so that we can receive something better.

Remember, Jesus claimed to be the Bread of Life, meaning He fills us, sustains us, and satisfies us. When we lay ourselves down, when we take up our cross, when we are crucified with Christ—we don't just give everything up for nothing! We are receiving something far greater and more fulfilling than sin and the world have to offer.

The old has gone, but praise God, the new has come! We are crucified with Christ, but Christ comes to live in us! We are never without help or hope.

"To them God has chosen to make known among the Gentiles the glorious riches of this mystery, which is Christ in you, the hope of glory" (Colossians 1:27).

Notice the first part of the definition of *abstain* is "to be distant, avoid, a way off, about seven miles." I actually laughed out loud the first time I read that last part in my concordance. The interesting thing about the definition is that in Hebrew culture, the number seven represents completeness. For instance, God rested on the seventh day of creation because His work was complete.

So, in the case of this definition, we can see that a *complete* separation from something that is causing us to sin is necessary in order to win this war for our souls. Our minds, wills, and emotions are constantly being bombarded with temptations to sin. We will never walk in God's will until we learn how to resist those temptations.

"No temptation has seized you except what is common to man. And God is faithful; he will not let you be tempted beyond what you can bear. But when you are tempted, he will also provide a way out so that you can stand up under it" (1 Corinthians 10:13).

God doesn't leave us to struggle with sin on our own. He gives His Holy Spirit to empower us to stand up under temptation. Together with the Spirit, we have to make the choice to take the way out that He gives us.

If we need to separate ourselves "about seven miles" from sin in order to walk in God's will and receive the fullness of all He has for us, then let's do it!

The key is to remember that we will walk in the fullness of God's will for our lives as we surrender our will to His. We are giving up the desires of our sinful nature in order to receive the blessing of walking with God, full of His joy and peace.

Our sinful nature doesn't just leave us at the moment we become Christians. We have to battle that nature, but we can make a decision that we would rather have what God wants for us than to enjoy the comfort and pleasures of sin.

The Enemy

Not only will we be tempted by our own fleshly desires, but our enemy, the devil, will also tempt us to *feed* our flesh or comfort our souls. In other words, he will place us in situations that tempt us to eat the wrong foods.

Satan is the enemy of God, which makes Him our enemy. His desire is to steal, kill, and destroy. He will use our flesh or physical appetites to tempt us.

"Be self-controlled and alert. Your enemy the devil prowls around like a roaring lion looking for someone to devour. Resist him, standing firm in the faith" (1 Peter 5:8).

We know what it is to be driven by the flesh—food, alcohol, sex, pride, judgment, gossip, anger, unforgiveness. When we give in to those temptations that feel good or make us feel better about ourselves, we aren't walking in the wisdom and will of God. We will have confusion, strife, and lack of direction for our lives.

Falling into these temptations is why so many people don't know God's will for their lives.

We need the mercy and grace of God to cover us and move us forward with Him. Though God is generous in His mercy and grace, this doesn't give us an excuse to be lazy about how we live. We are called to holiness.

"Therefore, prepare your minds for action; be self-controlled; set your hope on the grace to be given you when Jesus Christ is revealed. As obedient children, do not conform to the evil desires you had when you lived in ignorance. But just as he who called you is holy, so be holy in all you do" (1 Peter 1:13-15).

When we walk continually in sin with little regard for walking in the Spirit, we are missing out on God's best for our lives.

Let's look at three biblical examples of Satan tempting people with the wrong food.

In Genesis 3:1-6, Satan, in the form of a serpent, tempted Eve to disobey the instruction of God not to eat the fruit of the tree of the knowledge of good and evil. He tempted her with a question:

"He said to the woman, 'Did God really say, "You must not eat from any tree in the garden?"'" (Genesis 3:1b).

Satan put doubt into Eve's mind about what God had really said and why He said it. And because the fruit was "pleasing to the eye and desirable for gaining wisdom," Eve ate the fruit. She was feeding her flesh (eye) and her soul (wisdom).

In Exodus 16, the Israelites had been led out of slavery in Egypt and were being led by God, through Moses, into the Promised Land. Along the way, the people began to grumble because they couldn't find food to feed over two million people. So the Lord provided manna—bread from heaven—every single day to feed them.

But over in Numbers 11 we see the Israelites began complaining about the manna.

"The rabble with them began to crave other food, and again the Israelites started wailing and said, 'If only we had meat to eat! We remember the fish we ate in Egypt at no cost—also the cucumbers, melons, leeks, onions, and garlic. But now we have lost our appetite; we never see anything but this manna!'" (Numbers 11:4-6).

The Israelites had been fed daily by God's own hand, but the enemy (the rabble or non-Israelites who were mixed in among them) tempted them to "crave other food." And once again, we see people feeding their flesh, rather than being comforted and satisfied with what God had to offer.

We do the same thing. We listen to the lies of the enemy who tells us that what God offers isn't enough. We listen to his lie that causes us to doubt that God really wants to satisfy our hunger Himself. And we give in to the temptation to eat the wrong food.

Whether it's feeding our flesh with physical comforts or feeding our emotions with emotional comfort, we're still feeding on something that brings temporary pleasure but leaves us still longing for more.

But let's look at one more example.

"Jesus, full of the Holy Spirit, returned from the Jordan and was led by the Spirit in the desert, where for forty days he was tempted by the devil. He ate nothing during those days, and at the end of them he was hungry.

The devil said to him, 'If you are the Son of God, tell this stone to become bread'" (Luke 4:1-3).

Here we see another example of Satan using the temptation of the wrong food. Jesus truly is the Son of God. He could have turned the stone to bread if He wanted to. But it would have been the wrong food.

"Jesus answered, 'It is written: "Man does not live on bread alone"'" (Luke 4:4).

It is no coincidence in this passage that Jesus is quoting Deuteronomy 8:3, a passage in which Moses was teaching the Israelites not to seek after the wrong food, but to be satisfied with that which God provides:

"He humbled you, causing you to hunger and then feeding you with manna, which neither you nor your fathers had known, to teach you that man does not live on bread alone but on every word that comes from the mouth of the Lord."

The enemy knows how we want to fill our own hunger, and he's ready with the wrong food. But God has provided all that we need. When we surrender our lives to Him, He will satisfy us by His Spirit and His Word, as long as we continue to seek Him daily.

"O God, you are my God, earnestly I seek you; my soul thirsts for you, my body longs for you, in a dry and weary land where there is no water.

"I have seen you in the sanctuary and beheld your power and your glory. Because your love is better than life, my lips will glorify you. I will praise you as long as I live, and in your name I will lift up my hands. My soul will be satisfied as with the richest of foods; with singing lips my mouth will praise you" (Psalm 63:1-5).

In the next chapter, we will explore how to eat the right foods that will satisfy our souls. For now, think about these questions.

Is there ongoing sin in your life according to God's Word that you know you need to deal with?

What are the areas of temptation that you struggle with the most?

What seems to be the biggest obstacle you face in overcoming that struggle?

What would it look like for you to deal with that sin and overcome it?

Take a few minutes to ask God to help you identify and overcome these struggles.

I'll see you on the next page.

CHAPTER 5

FEED YOUR SPIRIT AND SATISFY YOUR SOUL

> "O God, I have tasted Thy goodness, and it has both satisfied me and made me thirsty for more."
> —A.W. Tozer

We learned in the last chapter that our flesh and our soul will constantly seek to be fed with the things that make us feel good. So often when we partake of these things, they leave us still hungry and unsatisfied, because we are filling up on the wrong things.

In this chapter, we will look at how we can feed ourselves the things that will truly satisfy.

New Creations

When we give our lives to Christ, we become a new creation with new desires that will begin to align with God and His Word.

"Therefore, if anyone is in Christ, he is a new creation; the old has gone, the new has come!" (2 Corinthians 5:17).

Jesus paid the price for our sin on the cross. In the divine exchange, He took on our sin, so we could take on His righteousness.

"God made him who had no sin to be sin for us, so that in him we might become the righteousness of God" (2 Corinthians 5:21).

We are made righteous through the blood of Jesus. This is called positional righteousness because it identifies our position before the Father. In His eyes, through Christ, we are righteous.

We are also growing in righteousness, day-by-day, as we grow in our relationship with the Lord. This is called progressive righteousness, as we work with the Holy Spirit to be conformed into the image of Christ. This is an ongoing process throughout our lifetime.

The Holy Spirit fills believers to lead us and guide us. We must choose—moment by moment, day by day—to make the decision to die to self and allow the Holy Spirit to be our guide.

"I have been crucified with Christ and I no longer live, but Christ lives in me. The life I live in the body, I live by faith in the Son of God, who loved me and gave himself for me" (Galatians 2:20).

If we really want to hear from God and walk in His will, we will have to learn how to feed our spirit the things that will encourage spiritual growth. We will have to learn how to guard against what we perceive—that means guarding the mind, emotions, and will against the things that don't feed our spirit, and instead seeking those things that bring real satisfaction to our souls.

Renew Your Mind in the Word

The battle begins in the mind where we process information. God's Word is full of instructions for how to deal with this battle.

"Those who live according to the sinful nature have their minds set on what that nature desires; but those who live in accordance with the Spirit have their minds set on what the Spirit desires. The mind of sinful man is death, but the mind controlled by the Spirit is life and peace" (Romans 8:5-6).

The first thing Scripture teaches us here is that we have to set our minds on what the Spirit desires and not on what our sinful nature desires. Just as we talked about in the last chapter, we must choose what we feed. If we feed our sinful nature—it will continue to demand more. The sinful nature is never satisfied.

But if we choose to feed the spirit—the part of us that connects with God's Spirit within—our spirit will be satisfied. In order to feed the spirit, we have to renew our minds, because what the Spirit of God desires is contrary to what our sinful nature desires.

"Therefore, I urge you, brothers, in view of God's mercy, to offer your bodies as living sacrifices, holy and pleasing to God—this is your spiritual act of worship. Do not conform any longer to the pattern of this world, but be transformed by the renewing of your mind. Then you will be able to test and approve what God's will is—his good, pleasing, and perfect will" (Romans 12:1-2).

This verse teaches us that as our minds are transformed and renewed in God's Word, we'll be able to test and know God's perfect will for our lives.

The more time we spend in God's Word, the more we feed our spirit what it really desires and what truly satisfies.

Psalm 119 is a Hebrew acrostic poem. Every eight-verse stanza begins with a succeeding letter of the Hebrew alphabet. What I love most is that all 176 verses contain a word that refers to the Word of God—words like law, statutes, precepts, ways, decrees, word, and commands. Every line reminds us of how the Word of God sustains, directs, guides, provides, encourages, rebukes, comforts, and fulfills.

Here are just a few examples. I encourage you to study it for yourself.

"I have hidden your word in my heart that I might not sin against you" (11).

"I run in the path of your commands, for you have set my heart free" (32).

"Your commands make me wiser than my enemies" (98).

"How sweet are your words to my taste, sweeter than honey to my mouth!" (103).

"Your word is a lamp for my feet and a light for my path." (105).

The Word is so important to our lives, that I can't possibly overstate it. The more we turn off the television, put down the phone, and guard our eyes and ears from the world's influence; and the more we will spend time with God, His Word, His music, His ways, the more we will know and understand God's will for our lives.

Living in God's will requires sacrifice, but it is so, so worth it!

When we notice thoughts that are contrary to God and His Word, we have to learn to capture those thoughts quickly and replace them with what is good and holy.

"We demolish arguments and every pretention that sets itself up against the knowledge of God, and we take captive every thought to make it obedient to Christ" (2 Corinthians 10: 5).

"Finally, brothers, whatever is true, whatever is noble, whatever is right, whatever is pure, whatever is lovely, whatever is admirable— if anything is excellent or praiseworthy—think about such things" (Philippians 4:8).

Remember that daily quiet time we talked about in the first section? That is your primary defense in learning to renew your mind in God's Word. We need to spend time in Bible study, Scripture memorization, and word studies on the areas we struggle with.

For example, if we struggle with pride, we need to study pride. If we struggle with unforgiveness, we need to study unforgiveness. The Word will work in our lives, but only to the extent that we put the Word to work in our lives.

As we renew our mind in the things of God, we will desire the things that satisfy the spirit rather than the flesh—Christian music, Christian books and magazines, Christian movies. Our hearts will begin to desire more and more of God and His ways.

"Delight yourself in the Lord and he will give you the desires of your heart" (Psalm 37:4).

Express Your Emotions in Worship

Another way we can feed our spirits is through worship. Emotions are not bad, but they should be a gauge, not a guide. In other words, we don't need to be led by our emotions; instead, we should allow our emotions to be expressed through our faith. The best way I have found to express my emotions is through worship.

God is an emotional God, and He made us in His image. When we express ourselves in worship as the Bible instructs, we will release emotions—we may cry, sing, lift our hands, shout, pray, or laugh— all during worship.

I'm not talking about being out of control in worship or being fake and just showing a bunch of emotion. I'm talking about entering a time of praise and worship in which we can express our emotions to God. I have worshiped when I was angry and felt the anger leave. I have worshiped when I was sad and had my sadness leave.

My father was a Vietnam veteran who suffered from PTSD. He became an alcoholic as a result, withdrew from family and friends, and left home when I was twelve. Many years later, after I was married and had children, he came back into our lives. I spent as much time with him as I could, trying to help him and lead him to the Lord.

During that time, my sister and I experienced many trials in dealing with his depression, addiction, and suicidal tendencies. Our children also endured the ups and downs of trying to get to know their grandfather who was so dysfunctional and broken.

On November 11, 2007, his body finally gave up, and his soul found rest in the arms of God. His salvation story is a rough, broken, and short road that left very little time for us to spend together as Christians on this earth, but an eternity forever with God.

I'll never forget the Sunday morning after his death. I was the worship leader in our church, and as we gathered to pray before our rehearsal that morning, one of the band members told me I didn't have to lead worship that morning. They all understood my grief.

I told them I was just really sad, but I still wanted to lead worship. So we took to the stage, and they pulled up the first song on the screen. I had planned worship some time the week before Daddy died, and didn't even remember what songs I had planned. The first one that popped up on the screen was this:

Trading My Sorrows[9]

We began to sing, and as those words came from my heart and through my lips, God lifted the sorrow and gave me His joy. All of the sadness I felt in that moment was released in my worship, directed to my God who understood, and released at His feet.

That's what worship does. We are able to express the deepest cry of our hearts in an appropriate way, which oftentimes will help us to not express our emotions in inappropriate ways, such as angry outbursts, anxiety, or depression.

In the Psalms, David often expressed anger, joy, sadness, rejoicing, and depression to God. By the time he finished releasing those emotions in worship, he was praising God.

If we will just be genuine with our worship and express our emotions appropriately, we will be less likely to express them inappropriately at other times and with other people.

Surrender Your Will through Obedience

To line up our will with God's will requires obedience. The more time we spend with God in His Word and in prayer, the more we will understand what that means.

Obedience is a key to knowing God's will for your life.

In the Garden of Gethsemane, Jesus was overwhelmed with sorrow and prayed to the Father:

"'Abba, Father,' he said, 'everything is possible for you. Take this cup from me. Yet not what I will, but what you will'" (Mark 14:36).

Jesus knew the suffering that He was about to endure on the cross—not only the physical pain, but also the rejection of the Father as He took on the weight of our sin. As Jesus bore our sins on the cross, the Father poured out His wrath toward sin on His Son. In the garden, His humanity struggled with the pain that lay before Him.

Yet, Jesus said in John 10:18 that He laid down His life of His own accord. It was Jesus' obedience to the Father that made a way for you and me to know Him.

"'If you love me, you will obey what I command'" (John 14:15).

"'Whoever has my commands and obeys them, he is the one who loves me. He who loves me will be loved by my Father, and I too will love him and show myself to him'" (John 14:21).

"Jesus replied, 'If anyone loves me, he will obey my teaching. My Father will love him, and we will come to him and make our home with him. He who does not love me will not obey my teaching. These words you hear are not my own; they belong to the Father who sent me'" (John 14:23-24).

Jesus Himself made it clear that the evidence of our love for God is our obedience. If we want to know God's will for our lives, we need to start by obeying His will as taught to us in His Word. If we will seek Him and humbly desire to live in obedience to His commands, He will guide us into His perfect will.

"Be joyful always; pray continually; give thanks in all circumstances, for this is God's will for you in Christ Jesus" (1 Thessalonians 5:16-18).

Be quick to recognize sin and turn away from it. He knows your heart and your willingness to seek Him and walk in His will. He delights in helping you to overcome. Be joyful, prayerful, and thankful.

Surrender completely—mind, will, emotions—and watch God work in you to do what you never could on your own.

"The one who calls you is faithful and he will do it" (1 Thessalonians 5:24).

When we learn how to starve our sinful nature what it craves (sin and comfort) and feed our spirit what it craves (the things of God), we will find that our soul (mind, will, emotions) is satisfied.

Your spirit longs for the Bread of life. Feed it.

As you begin this journey toward God's will, you will be faced with a spiritual battle. Satan doesn't want you to obey God or walk in His will, and he will pull out the tools of his arsenal to fight against your progress towards righteousness. In the next chapter we will talk about spiritual warfare.

First, let's think about a few things.

What are some areas of perception you need to guard against, such as music, social media, television, etc.?

How can you make a change in one area of renewing your mind this week?

Do you express your emotions often in worship? Why or why not?

Is there an area of obedience that you are struggling with right now? Do a word study on that topic and ask the Lord to give you His power to overcome.

CHAPTER 6

USE SPIRITUAL WEAPONS TO FIGHT SPIRITUAL BATTLES

"We are evidently no friends
of Satan. Like the kings of this world,
he wars not against his own subjects.
The very fact that he assaults us
should fill our minds with hope."
—J.C. Ryle

The more we seek God, the more of Himself He will reveal to us.
The more He reveals to us, the more the enemy will try to steal
from us. In the last chapter, I mentioned that Satan wants to tempt
us to satisfy our own hunger with what the world has to offer.

"The thief comes only to steal, kill, and destroy; I have come that they may have life, and have it to the full" (John 10:10).

Satan will also use circumstances and other people to cause us stress, despair, anxiety, fear, unforgiveness, strife, doubt, and anything that keeps us out of the will of God for our lives.

We have to remember in these situations that our battle is not against people, but a spiritual battle that must be fought with spiritual weapons.

"For our struggle is not against flesh and blood, but against the rulers, against the authorities, against the powers of this dark world and against the spiritual forces of evil in the heavenly realms" (Ephesians 5:12).

Satan is a created being, a fallen angel. He isn't the antithesis of God, the opposite of God, or the bad to God's good. He doesn't even register that high on the meter.

God is an uncreated Being, who was, and is, and is to come. Satan was created by God, so he can't be God's opposite.

He does have power, but his power is under the authority of Almighty God.

Jesus defeated Satan on the cross.

"And having disarmed the powers and authorities, he made a public spectacle of them, triumphing over them by the cross" (Colossians 2:15).

"The reason the Son of God appeared was to destroy the devil's work" (1 John 3:8b).

We are seated with Jesus in high places.

"And God raised us up with Christ and seated us with him in the heavenly realms in Christ Jesus" (Ephesians 2:6).

Our job is to take our place and believe what God's word says about us and about the enemy.

"Submit yourselves, then, to God. Resist the devil, and he will flee from you" (James 4:7).

If we draw near to God and resist the devil, he will flee. Don't give a foothold to the devil and his deceptions. He is the father of lies.

"He was a murderer from the beginning, not holding to the truth, for there is no truth in him. When he lies, he speaks his native language, for he is a liar and the father of lies" (John 8:44b).

So, how do we deal with the attacks, the trials, and the problems that we face as a result of his attacks?

I want you to read the story of Jehoshaphat. No, seriously. Put down this book and turn to 2 Chronicles 20 and read this story.

Jehoshaphat was one of the kings of Judah who was striving to follow the Lord and do what was right (2 Chronicles 17:3). Then a vast army came against him to make war on Jehoshaphat and his people. As I shared at the beginning of this chapter, it is often when we are striving to do what is right that Satan creeps in to cause us problems. Let's look at how he responded to this attack from the enemy.

From this story I see five keys to breakthrough that we can use to open the door to the blessings of God and the spirit of overcoming the enemy.

Fasting

The first thing Jehoshaphat did was proclaim a fast.

"Alarmed, Jehoshaphat resolved to inquire of the LORD, and he proclaimed a fast for all Judah" (2 Chronicles 20:3).

Fasting is a means of seeking God through self-denial of food. It's a way of being set apart unto God and saying to God that we want nothing—not even food—but to hear His voice and know His will.

There are different examples of fasting in the Bible, but they all involve giving up food for a particular time. Daniel fasted choice meats and wine. Esther proclaimed a fast before going before the king. In Matthew 6:16, Jesus said, "When you fast" not "if you fast," so Jesus expected that His followers would fast at some point.

In Acts, the early church would fast and pray for direction and for the Holy Spirit to lead them when choosing leaders (Acts 13:2-3).

Jehoshaphat proclaimed a fast for all of Judah, so the people could consecrate or set themselves apart as unto the Lord. Fasting releases God's power in our lives because it is a way of declaring that we are totally dependent upon Him.

Fasting says to God that we need Him more than food.

Prayer

Next, Jehoshaphat led the entire assembly of Judah in prayer. It was a prayer of praise and thanks to God for Who He is, acknowledging His divine sovereignty over them. It was a prayer reminding God of all He had promised them in the past. It was a prayer asking God to show them what to do. It was also a prayer of complete humility and dependence upon God to help them.

This prayer demonstrates the heart of one who is completely surrendered to God and trusting in Him for the answer. All of Judah came and participated in this prayer, from the "children and little ones" to the wives and the men.

If we want God to help us stand against the enemy, we must acknowledge Him as the only source of our help. We need to stop talking about the problem to people and just go to God. The Holy Spirit is our Counselor.

"But the Counselor, the Holy Spirit, whom the Father will send in my name, will teach you all things and will remind you of everything I have said to you" (John 14:26).

We must also pray for those we consider our enemies, remembering that our real enemy is the devil who is using them.

"But I tell you: Love your enemies and pray for those who persecute you" (Matthew 5:44).

We must pray with faith and with boldness, believing that God hears our prayers and will answer according to His will and His Word.

The Word

After Jehoshaphat prayed, the Spirit of the LORD came upon one of the priests, who then shared the Word of the LORD with them (20:14-17). God spoke through Him and gave Him the exact instructions for what they were to do.

We have the written Word of God to direct us into the truth in every situation. God will speak if we will get our minds off our problem and focus on Him. We can pray God's Word back to Him and remind Him of His promises to us.

There is so much power in speaking God's Word.

"As the rain and the snow come down from heaven, and do not return to it without watering the earth and making it bud and flourish, so that it yields seed for the sower and bread for the eater, so is my word that goes out from my mouth: it will not return to me empty, but will accomplish what I desire and achieve the purpose for which I sent it" (Isaiah 55:10-11).

When we are going through a spiritual battle, we need to look up Scriptures that speak truth over our situation and confess those words aloud. Our words have creative power. Just as God spoke the world into existence, our words can change the atmosphere over which we speak them.

"The LORD said to me, 'You have seen correctly, for I am watching to see that my word is fulfilled'" (Jeremiah 1:12).

"The tongue has the power of life and death, and those who love it will eat its fruit" (Proverbs 18:22).

Our words can also have negative power, if we are agreeing with our circumstances instead of agreeing with God. Guard your tongue from confessing anything but God's truth in your life.

Worship

My favorite part of this story is that Jehoshaphat sent the praise team out at the head of the army!

Not the soldiers with shields, swords, or bows. No, the singers and those with instruments.

"After consulting the people, Jehoshaphat appointed men to sing to the LORD and praise him for the splendor of his holiness as they went out at the head of the army, saying: 'Give thanks to the LORD, for his love endures forever'" (2 Chronicles 20:21).

Oh, the power of praise and worship! You see, they fasted to let the Lord know they were serious; they consulted with the Lord through prayer; then the Word of the Lord came to them with a strategy for breakthrough. They were told to go out and face the enemy because God would be with them. They were told to take up their positions and stand firm. Their response to God's Word? Worship.

"Jehoshaphat bowed with his face to the ground, and all the people of Judah and Jerusalem fell down in worship before the LORD" (2 Chronicles 20:18).

We see another example of this in the Bible when Paul and Silas were thrown in jail.

"At midnight Paul and Silas were praying and singing hymns to God, and the other prisoners were listening to them. Suddenly there was such a violent earthquake that the foundations of the prison doors were shaken. At once all the prison doors flew open, and everybody's chains came loose" (Acts 16:25-26).

Paul and Silas chose not to focus on their desperate situation. Instead, they focused on God and His power. Not only were they freed, but so were all those around them.

Worship takes the focus off us and our problems and puts it on the only One who can do anything about our situation. Jehoshaphat was faced with an army that outnumbered him. His only hope was in the Lord. By sending the praise team out at the head of the army, he was declaring his total dependence on God for the victory.

When we are in a spiritual battle, it's hard not to complain or be upset. If we can get our hearts focused on God and who He is and all He can do, it releases our faith to let God act on our behalf.

There is one more aspect to spiritual breakthrough.

Obedience

Obedience is probably the hardest of the keys to breakthrough, but it is the most essential. Our obedience shows God that we are willing to do whatever He asks of us. It shows that we are sincere in our desire to please Him.

In Jehoshaphat's story, the people did everything God asked them to do. "Early in the morning" they set out, they listened to their leader as he gave the instructions from the Lord, and they "began to sing and praise." As they did, the Lord set ambushes against Jehoshaphat's enemies, and they destroyed each other in the confusion.

Not only did they overcome, but because of their obedience, no one could get the glory but God! The praise team couldn't get the credit—they had no weapons. The army couldn't get the credit—they didn't kill anybody. Only God could get the credit because Jehoshaphat's enemies got confused and turned on each other.

Many times when we are in a battle, God will speak to us and give us a strategy for victory. It may include worship and prayer, but it may also be something that requires complete trust in Him, such as forgiving someone who has hurt us or giving up something we really like.

I was going through a tough time recently and God impressed on my heart to reach out to someone I may have offended. The truth is that I didn't really know if I had offended her or not, but I knew God wanted me to make it right no matter what.

I had to get really sick and desperate before I listened to the Lord and did what He said, because I was afraid that I really had offended her, and it would open up something with which I didn't want to deal. Even so, in my desperation, I contacted her. I was relieved to learn that all was well. I just had to be obedient.

When we get serious about spiritual warfare and realize that our weapons are spiritual and not carnal or physical, then we can fight with spiritual tools. That's how we overcome. This truth will be of great importance as we seek to walk in God's will.

Satan's desire is to keep us so distracted and worried and fearful and mad and upset about anything he can get our focus on, that we will not be able to walk in God's will for our lives. The good news is we don't have to succumb to his lies and distractions. We can walk in victory.

Stay in the Word, in prayer, in worship, in obedience, and fast when necessary. The enemy will flee and you will be released to keep moving forward in what God has called you to do.

It may take some time, but God is always on time.

You know what the best part of this story is? When the battle was over, Jehoshaphat and his men went to see what had happened, and all they saw were the bodies of their enemies. They carried off so much plunder, it took them three days to do it (20:24-25)!

God will not only come through for us when we follow these five keys to breakthrough, but he will also bless us for putting Him first through fasting, prayer, His Word, worship, and obedience.

Jehoshaphat and his men were so blessed that the fear of their God came upon all their enemies.

"And the kingdom of Jehoshaphat was at peace, for his God had given him rest on every side" (20:30).

Rest on every side. How's that for the blessings of obedience?

The last chapter in this section is on walking in God's will. Before we move forward, let's pause and answer a few questions.

What has the enemy used to keep you distracted from doing God's will?

What spiritual weapons (the five keys) do you feel you are weakest in right now?

What can you do to turn up the heat and go into battle-mode against the enemy?

Spend a few minutes with God to seek His help in growing in that area.

CHAPTER 7

KEEP YOUR EYES
ON THE FINISH LINE

> **"The will of God will not
> take us where the grace of
> God cannot sustain us."
> —Billy Graham**

A few years ago, I wrote a Bible study called *Let's Run! Running the Race with Faith and Perseverance*. It's a study of the heroes of the faith in Hebrews chapter 11 and the call to run our race with faith in Hebrews 12:1-3.

"Therefore, since we are surrounded by such a great cloud of witnesses, let us throw off everything that hinders and the sin that so easily entangles, and let us run with perseverance the race marked out for us. Let us fix our eyes on Jesus, the author and perfecter of our faith, who for the joy set before him endured the cross, scorning its shame, and sat down at the right hand of the throne of God. Consider him who endured such opposition from sinful men, so that you will not grow weary and lose heart" (Hebrews 12:1-3).

When God gave me this passage to study, I had no idea it would lead to writing a book. I just wanted to study the passage and lead my students at school in the study as well. The next thing I knew, God was calling me to write a book and run in a 5-K!

Listen, I don't run. I don't mind walking for exercise or even lifting a few weights. But I don't like to run. At all. So when I felt God was telling me to do this, I ignored His voice for a while before I realized I would be disobedient if I didn't do this thing.

I downloaded an app on my phone to help me slowly be able to go from not exercising to being able to run a 5-K in just a few weeks. I will tell you now. It was awful. Some days I cried. Some days, I dragged myself down our dirt road in an effort to stay faithful to the task.

There were days that my legs felt like lead. It seemed I would never get to the point where it was easy. But eventually that day did come. Actually, it was at night. I had gotten home late from school, but I had a commitment to run on certain days as part of my training. It was already dark outside, but I got my shoes on and set my playlist on my phone and started running.

After a while, I was thinking what a beautiful night it was, the moon was shining brightly, and my favorite song was playing. I suddenly realized, "Hey! I feel good! This actually feels good!!"

It wasn't hurting; I wasn't out of breath; I actually felt as if I could keep going for a long time.

Living the Christian life is a lot like training for a race.

"Do you not know that in a race all the runners run, but only one gets the prize? Run in such a way as to get the prize. Everyone who competes in the games goes into strict training. They do it to get a crown that will not last; but we do it to get a crown that will last forever" (1 Corinthians 9:24-25).

The prize is eternity. And, no, we can't do anything to earn it, but we do have to stay in the race. We have to keep our eyes on the prize.

Spiritual Discipline

First, we have to train ourselves in the things of God. We never arrive or know it all. We are daily being conformed into His image as we seek Him through prayer and the Word. Our training takes place through church, Bible studies, our daily quiet time, and the counsel of older, wiser Christians in our lives.

Some days, the discipline of spending time with the Lord or going to church will feel like a burden. We have to persevere through those days, remembering our Savior and all He has done for us. Just as I pushed through to train on those late nights or cold nights when I didn't want to, God wants us to follow through on our commitments to Him.

It does get easier and better with time. Soon, we will be really excited about our time with the Lord and look forward to it.

Second, we have to deal with the hindrances and the sin that will cause us to stray off track. Hindrances can be anything the enemy uses to keep our eyes off Jesus—even good things. Sin is anything in our lives that doesn't please God. We deal with both of these by spending time with God every day and asking Him to cleanse us.

It's also good to do a check every now and then to make sure we don't have something in our lives that we are blind to.

"Examine yourselves to see whether you are in the faith; test yourselves" (2 Corinthians 13:5).

In other words, ask God to examine your heart and mind and show you anything that is not of Him. Then be sure to deal with it through repentance. We have to completely turn away from all sin and allow the Holy Spirit to fill us.

"If we confess our sins, he is faithful and just and will forgive us our sins and purify us from all unrighteousness" (1 John 1:9).

Third, we have to keep our eyes on Jesus and eternity. Some of the things we struggle with in this life aren't even all that important in light of eternity. We need to ask God to give us an eternal perspective. That's how the heroes in Hebrews 11 were able to keep the faith.

"He has made everything beautiful in its time. He has also set eternity in the hearts of men" (Ecclesiastes 3:11).

Eternity is in our hearts. Deep down, it's what we all long for. If we keep our focus on what we are achieving by being faithful to God, day in and day out, it will be much easier.

"And without faith it is impossible to please God, because anyone who comes to him must believe that he exists and that he rewards those who earnestly seek him" (Hebrews 11:6).

Perseverance

Discipline is always difficult at first, but it does get easier with time. When I had hard days training, I would remember two things: I had made a commitment to the Lord and I wanted to see it through. I also wanted to know what it felt like to complete the race. I knew if I gave up training, I would never get to experience the finish line.

I know a 5-K probably isn't that big of a deal, but to me it was huge. I had never done anything like that before. On the night of the event, the weather was perfect. It was in November, but only in the low 50's. The race took us through a nice neighborhood in which all the homes were decorated for Christmas. It was just beautiful.

I was able to run the entire race without stopping, and my husband ran with me the whole way. Just the two of us. And Jesus.

When I crossed that line, my children waiting for me on the other side, you would have thought I had won the Boston Marathon. I was a hero, like those heroes of Hebrews 11. I had persevered in something difficult, because I was determined to do so.

God honored my obedience, my desire to please Him, and my determination to not give up.

I hope that you will be inspired to run your race for God with faith and passion. There is nothing like walking with God in obedience, even in the hard times. He gives us the peace and the joy of knowing that we are walking in His will.

I know many people feel that they don't know what God's will is for their lives. Maybe that was you when you downloaded this book. Maybe you desperately want to know God's will and you don't know how. All I can say is that when I am walking in obedience to the Lord, He always shows me the way. I may not know that I'm walking in it, but I can always look back and see that I am.

"Whether you turn to the right or to the left, your ears will hear a voice behind you, saying, 'This is the way; walk in it'" (Isaiah 30:21).

If you are struggling to make a decision or to know what God is calling you to do, may I suggest that you just seek Him for who He is and nothing else. Just do like Jehoshaphat and worship, or like Paul and Silas, sing a song to Him.

Just find Him in that secret place and tell Him. Don't try to hide anything (He sees it all anyway). Don't hold anything back from God. He knows you. He loves you. He has a plan for your life. He wants you to walk in His will more than you want it for yourself. He's not trying to hide it from you or hold anything back from you.

He just wants you.

We have to discipline ourselves. We have to be willing to let go of the sins and hindrances. We can't put ourselves and our own desires first and then expect God to get on board with our plans. He doesn't work that way.

Ask yourself what might be in the way of your being able to hear from God or know His will for your life. Sometimes we just have so many distractions in our lives that we are confused by the many voices. Get alone with God and turn off every other voice but His.

Too often, we use time as an excuse. I've often said I didn't have time to do something, but when I really look at my time, I waste so much of it.

We need to get beyond a lazy, slothful attitude and be determined to seek after the things of God with everything within us. If we want to hear from Him and walk in His will, then we have to surrender all that we are to Him and let Him have His way with us.

The time that we commit to Him is never wasted. It's worth it to spend time with Him, to grow in Him, and to enjoy the pleasure of knowing Him. And there's always more to learn. He is a never-ending Source of wisdom, love, understanding, growth, peace—all the things we need most in our lives. All can be found in Him.

God is a good Father to us. He will give us what we need, and as we delight ourselves in Him, He will place His desires in us and give us the desires of our hearts.

We won't walk in His truth or enjoy His presence if we live for self. We have to trust Him enough to lay down our own will and our own desires and seek Him first. As we do, He will meet us right where we are.

Max Lucado once said that God accepts us as we are, but He loves us too much to leave us there. Walking in His will includes learning what is right and what is wrong and seeking to honor Him with our lives.

So don't wallow in guilt and self-condemnation, but don't be lazy either. Let's stay in the middle of the road where we seek His will and walk in His ways, repenting and turning from sin when we fail.

His grace is sufficient. So, let's throw aside everything that hinders and the sin that entangles, and let's run!

Think on these questions:

What hinders you from running your race?

What sins have you entangled right now?

How can you throw aside the hindrances and sins and get back in the race with God?

What step can you take right now to refocus on the Lord?

The Bible study *Let's Run* has been revised and republished as *Living Faith: A Study of Hebrews 11*. You can order a copy here: www.amazon.com/Living-Faith-Study-Hebrews-11/dp/1732337675

SECTION 3

HOW TO CHANGE
YOUR WORLD

CHAPTER 8

START WHERE YOU ARE

> **"All great change in America
> begins at the dinner table."
> —Ronald Reagan**

When I was in college—before Jesus—I wanted to join the Peace Corps. I was studying elementary education, and I could think of nothing better than to spend my days in a one-room school in a remote village of Africa.

I think I came from the womb with a desire to make a difference. I've just always thought we were put here for more than just eating, sleeping, and breathing.

By the time I came into a personal relationship with Jesus, I was ready to conquer the world. I was also in love, so Africa got moved to the back burner, and marriage took priority.

We are all called to *be* disciples—fully devoted followers or learners.

"Therefore go and make disciples, baptizing them in the name of the Father and of the Son and of the Holy Spirit, and teaching them to obey everything I have commanded you. And surely I am with you always, to the very end of the age" (Matthew 28:19-20).

We are all called to *make* disciples. That's the bottom line. That's how I came to know the Lord and grow in Him—somebody took the time to disciple me. I heard recently that we are supposed to be "disciples, making disciple-making disciples."

Isn't that so cool?

Becoming a believer only reaffirmed my desire to change the world. Only now I had a message and a new mission: my home.

Change Your Home, Change Your World

You may be asking, "What does seeking God first have to do with changing your world?"

The simple answer is that as we begin to seek God first, He will send us out. He will place a desire in our hearts to share His love with those around us.

There are so many ways to serve the Lord, but the first and most important place is in our home. I realize everyone who reads this book may not be married. If you are single and live alone, think about your immediate family and those closest to you.

If you are married, your first responsibility in discipleship is your spouse.

Men are called to minister to their wives.

"Husbands, love your wives, just as Christ loved the church and gave himself up for her to make her holy, cleansing her by the washing with water through the word, and to present her to himself as a radiant church, without stain or wrinkle, or any other blemish, but holy and blameless. In this same way, husbands ought to love their wives as their own bodies. He who loves his wife loves himself" (Ephesians 5:25-28).

Women are called to minister to their husbands.

"Wives, submit to your husbands as to the Lord. For the husband is the head of the wife as Christ is the head of the church, his body, of which he is the Savior. Now as the church submits to Christ, so also wives should submit to their husbands in everything" (Ephesians 5:22-24).

I realize these aren't popular verses, but they are important. We can argue about what the Holy Spirit meant when these words were penned, but I think we can agree that husbands are to minister to their wives by loving them and teaching them the Word. Their role is to lead their wives by example, as Christ did, and to encourage them to be holy.

Wives are to submit to the leadership of their husbands, as their husbands lead by Christ's example. I always tell men (who complain that their wives don't want to submit to them), that if they will love their wives as Christ loved the church (sacrificially), their wives will gladly submit to their authority.

So, if we are married, and we want to know how to change our world for the kingdom, we can start by loving our spouses well. Build them up and encourage them in the Word of God.

If you have a spouse who is an unbeliever, then live your life as an example before him or her.

"Wives, in the same way be submissive to your husbands, so that, if any of them do not believe the word, they may be won over without words by the behavior of their wives, when they see the purity and reverence of your lives" (1 Peter 3:1-2).

We can encourage our spouses in discipleship by having devotions together, reading Scripture, and praying together. We can leave notes with Scriptures to encourage each other. We can guard our marriages by guarding our hearts, eyes, and ears from anything that would lead us astray.

We need to guard against close relationships with members of the opposite sex. If we are having problems with our spouse, we need to go to him or her prayerfully and respectfully and talk about it. We should never speak negatively about our spouse in front of others.

I'm not talking about abusive situations. I'm talking about a marriage in which we have disagreements and need to work things out. It's normal for husbands and wives to not agree about everything. The important thing is to talk to each other and not someone else. If you are in an abusive marriage, please seek help from a professional.

Parents are called to minister to their children and train them up in the instruction of the Lord.

"These commandments that I give you today are to be upon your hearts. Impress them on your children. Talk about them when you sit at home and when you walk along the road, when you lie down and when you get up" (Deuteronomy 6:6-7).

"Train a child in the way he should go, and when he is old he will not turn from it" (Proverbs 22:6).

Our children are our treasure. They're our first little disciples.

We can train our children by teaching them God's Word from a very early age. Read devotions with them and pray for them at bedtime. Have family dinner as many nights of the week as possible at the table with no television or cell phones allowed.

That almost sounds old-fashioned these days, and maybe it is. But I sure don't regret a single night we spent at our table, sharing and talking and praying together.

As parents, we are responsible for our children's spiritual training—not the church or the Christian school. The Bible gives us that responsibility.

There are many more verses about marriage and parenting, but the point is that oftentimes we are trying to find God's will for us in ministry, while ignoring our greatest calling right under our roof. Our own home and family should be the first place of ministry for each of us.

When it comes to changing your world, the first place to start is your inner circle of influence, which would be your home. As you seek God each day, He will lead you to be on mission with Him to make disciples—starting under your roof.

Change Your Workplace, Change Your World

Your next circle is your workplace if you work outside the home. Depending upon your vocation, you could have the opportunity to witness to many unbelievers every day. So often, we're asking God to give us a ministry, but we work side by side with people who need the Lord.

Jesus would consider that an awesome opportunity!

The best witness to unbelievers is love.

"By this all men will know that you are my disciples, if you love one another" (John 13:35).

We have to walk the talk and live what we confess. We can't talk about the Lord and our church, and live contradictory to what God's Word teaches. We aren't perfect, but as the Holy Spirit told me one time, "Live above reproach." In other words,

"Live such good lives among the pagans that, though they accuse you of doing wrong, they may see your good deeds and glorify God on the day he visits us" (1 Peter 2:12).

We do have a responsibility to guard our integrity because we represent the Lord in all we say and do. We need to have a joyful disposition, a peaceful attitude, and Spirit-filled speech.

So what do we do when we blow it? Just own it.

Most people will respect a Christian who strives to live above reproach, but is willing to humble herself and own her mistakes.

Of course, you will always experience those who are against you because of what you believe, but we have the power of prayer and the God of the universe on our side, so don't sweat it.

Pray for them and love them until they ask you why. Then share Jesus with them, disciple them, and bring them into your church.

Change Your Church, Change Your World

We also have a circle of influence within our church family. The same applies at church as in the workplace. We should seek each day to live by the Spirit and not the flesh, so that we can let our light shine everywhere we go. Church is no exception.

But I will admit, it's sometimes the hardest place to shine.

I've found that if I will spend time with the Lord before I go to church, I'll be less likely to get caught up in controversies, gossip, or negativity. The building we go to is just that: a building. We are the church, and God has given us many examples of the early church in Scripture.

"They broke bread in their homes and ate together with glad and sincere hearts, praising God and enjoying the favor of all the people" (Acts 2:46b).

If we have the right attitude, our church can be an awesome opportunity to make disciples. The church is a body of believers, but each one is at a different level of discipleship. We are all at some place of growing in our relationship with the Lord, from the newest Christian to the pastor.

We should have someone more mature in the faith from whom we can learn, and we should be discipling someone younger in the faith as well.

Paul and Timothy are an excellent example of discipleship. The letters of 1 and 2 Timothy were written by Paul to Timothy as Timothy was left to care for the church at Ephesus. In these letters we see the bond between the two, as Paul poured into Timothy's life, encouraging and teaching him.

"Timothy, guard what has been entrusted to your care. Turn away from godless chatter and the opposing ideas of what is falsely called knowledge, which some have professed and in so doing have wandered from the faith. Grace be with you" (1 Timothy 6:20-21).

Change Your Community, Change Your World

We also have a circle of influence in our community. From the post office to the market to the schoolhouse to the coffee house, we encounter people every day who need a growing, personal relationship with Jesus Christ.

Everywhere we go, we have the opportunity to show love to others. We can be loving, joyful, peaceful, patient, good, kind, gentle, faithful, and self-controlled. Those fruits of the Spirit are a tremendous witness to unbelievers—a whole lot more than just inviting them to church.

Sharing the Gospel is about building relationships with people. Discipleship is about doing life together in a way that shows (not just tells) us how to apply the Word to our lives.

If we just find one person in our community and begin to pray for her and build a relationship with her, I believe God will do the rest. He will work in that person's heart and lead us in our conversations until we have an open door to share the Gospel with her.

Because the Gospel involves recognizing and confessing and turning away from sin, I've found that telling someone that truth works much better when I have earned the right to share it by first investing in her as a person.

We have so many opportunities to share the Word with others and make a difference in our world. The best way is to just start where you are.

Think about these questions:

Where are you right now? Physically, emotionally, spiritually?

Who are the people in your circle of influence, starting with your family, co-workers, church, and community?

Who is discipling you?

Whom are you discipling?

For whom can you begin praying and building a relationship with right now?

These are the disciple-making disciples Jesus has given you. Stop and pray right now that God will move in their hearts and give you the opportunity to share His love and His truth with them.

CHAPTER 9

USE YOUR GIFTS

> "The world asks, 'What does
> a man own?' Christ asks,
> 'How does he use it?'"
> —Andrew Murray

When I first became a Christ-follower, I had really been touched by a girl I heard singing in one of my first church experiences as an adult. She had such a beautiful countenance and just exuded peace. I didn't really understand what she had, but I knew it was something I wanted. Not long after hearing her, I gave my life to the Lord.

I love to sing, and I naturally believed God was going to use me in music ministry, and He has. I've led choirs and sung on praise teams almost the entire time I've been a Christian. But I didn't stop there. I asked God to show me the gifts He's given for me to serve Him and build His Kingdom.

There are so many ways that we can serve God, in our homes, churches, and communities, but many people get hung up on trying to figure out what their gifts are.

I believe there is a difference between gifts and talents, and both should be used for the Lord. For instance, singing is a talent, not a spiritual gift as listed in the Bible. We use our voices in worship to serve God, but we also have actual spiritual gifts that we use within the Body of Christ.

"All of these [gifts] are the work of one and the same Spirit, and he gives them to each one, just as he determines" (1 Corinthians 12:11).

"We have different gifts, according to the grace given us" (Romans 12:6).

There are spiritual gift inventories you can take to assess your spiritual gifts if you are not sure, but you can be sure of this: you do have a gift, probably more than one.

"Now to each one the manifestation of the Spirit is given for the common good" (1 Corinthians 12:7).

These inventories will ask you a series of questions that will determine your natural bent and heart toward ministry. Your answers will guide you to a particular set of gifts and help determine how you can best use those gifts in ministry.

Here is a spiritual gift assessment by Lifeway that may be helpful to you: www.lifeway.com/Article/women-leadership-spiritual-gifts-growth-service.

Just Do Something

I'll tell you what I believe is the best way to determine your spiritual gifts: Just do something.

When I first began to serve in our church, I signed up for the nursery. After a few crying babies that I was terrified to hold and didn't know how to handle, I realized quickly that God hadn't gifted me to minister to babies.

Some people have that gift called "workers of miracles" (1 Corinthians 12:10) and *love* working in the nursery.

Seriously, there are those whom God has anointed to care for babies and minister the presence of God to them. That's awesome and I believe a great ministry for young moms and dads to be able to worship for an hour or two without any distractions.

Once I realized that was not my calling, I tried something else. The bottom line is that the best way to figure out what God has called you to do is to step out and try something. Don't be afraid of failure, and don't be afraid to say no.

When each person in the Body is fulfilling his call, the Church works like a fine-oiled machine. When you are functioning in the anointing of God for what He has called you to do, you will know it. It may not even be something you ever thought you would do or like, but there is a grace and anointing to do it.

1 Corinthians 12 teaches us about different spiritual gifts and how they work together within the body of Christ. Each gift is given by the same Spirit. He knows how to bring together a group of people

whose gifts will complement one another. When each of us is serving where and how we should, the body functions to carry out the mission of God.

"The body is a unit, though it is made up of many parts; and though all its parts are many, they form one body. So it is with Christ" (1 Corinthians 12:12).

Think about the natural talents you have as well, such as musical talents or writing or working with electronics. Talk to your pastor for wisdom and guidance. Then just step out and try something.

Remember, not all ministry will take place in your church. Some of the most effective ministry I take part in is online through my daily posts to Instagram and Facebook and my weekly blog. The Bible study that meets in my home each week is made up of ladies from various churches and some who aren't in church at all.

Just Be Faithful

Serve where you are and use what you have. Remember, little is much when God is in it. Just be faithful.

We don't all have to have the same gifts, and we shouldn't be envious of those who have better-looking or more appealing gifts. Every part is important.

"The eye cannot say to the hand, 'I don't need you!' And the head cannot say to the feet, 'I don't need you!' On the contrary, those parts of the body that seem to be weaker are indispensable . . ." (1 Corinthians 12:21-22).

"Now you are the body of Christ, and each one of you is a part of it" (1 Corinthians 12:27).

We are all part of the body, and every part is essential. So if I have a gift, but I'm not using it, something is missing within the body. If I'm not faithful to serve with my gifts, some mission of God is not being carried out.

It matters not how large or small our gift may seem. If we want to change our world, we need to be faithful to what God has gifted us to do. If God has called you to minister to babies in the nursery, don't feel that you can't change your world with that.

You may be rocking and singing to the next Billy Graham.

Every person's part is important to the body of Christ. We have to stop comparing our gifts and calling to someone else's. God has given me a big mouth. I write, teach, and speak, often in front of lots of people. That doesn't make my calling any better or more life-changing than yours.

Those who have the gift of faith and spend their time praying behind the scenes are the real world-changers. Those with the gift of helping others, who come alongside and encourage, who function in the gifts of service and hospitality—these are just as important to changing our world as the leaders, administrators, and evangelists.

If you truly want to change your world, start right where you are. Use whatever God has placed in your hands. Function in the talents and gifts that draw you into that place of grace so that only He gets the glory.

Even the trials and experiences that are difficult can be used by God to minister to someone else. God doesn't waste anything. He just needs willing hearts who will cooperate with His Holy Spirit and go where He sends.

As we head into our last chapter, take a minute to consider the following:

Have you ever taken a spiritual gifts inventory?

If so, what did you identify as your spiritual gifts?

If not, what do you think are your spiritual gifts?

What are some of your natural talents?

How are you currently serving the Lord, whether at home, at church, or in your community?

What steps do you need to take to be more faithful with the talents and gifts God has given you?

CHAPTER 10

TURN YOUR WORLD
UPSIDE DOWN

> "Catch on fire with enthusiasm
> and people will come for
> miles to watch you burn."
> —Charles Wesley

As I was sitting here writing this, I picked up my phone for a minute and came across a post from a friend. She is someone that I helped to disciple several years ago. She has come so far with the Lord and is serving Him today.

Her post was of her brother who has now given *his* life to the Lord and was singing a worship song. Disciples making disciple-making disciples. I just shed a few tears.

You know, you could live your whole life as a believer in Jesus Christ but never do anything of value to build the kingdom. Sure, you can go to church, pay your tithes, pray, read your Bible, and even love God. But Jesus said something that stands out to me today as I write this:

"If you love me, you will obey what I command" (John 14:15).

Then there's this command:

"Therefore go and make disciples of all nations, baptizing them in the name of the Father and of the Son and of the Holy Spirit, teaching them to obey everything I have commanded you. And surely I am with you always, to the very end of the age" (Matthew 28:19-20).

"He said to them, 'Go into all the world and preach the good news to all creation'" (Mark 16:15).

Did you get that?

It's hard to say that we love Jesus if we don't obey His command to make disciples—even when it's hard, even if we're uncomfortable, even if it costs us.

The followers of Jesus faced persecution, jail, and even death because they shared the good news of what Jesus had done in their lives.

In Acts 17, Paul and Silas had just been miraculously released from jail after being imprisoned for casting a demon out of a girl, and they were then asked to leave the city. They left Philippi and went to Thessalonica, where they continued to share the good news and make disciples.

"But the Jews were jealous; so they rounded up some bad characters from the marketplace, formed a mob and started a riot in the city. They rushed to Jason's house in search of Paul and Silas in order to bring them out to the crowd. But when they did not find them, they dragged Jason and some other brothers before the city officials, shouting: 'These men who have caused trouble all over the world have now come here'" (Acts 17:5-6).

I want you to see that last verse again, but in the King James Version:

"And when they found them not, they drew Jason and certain brethren unto the rulers of the city, crying, These that have turned the world upside down are come hither also (Acts 17:6, KJV).

You see, there are those who sit in the pew and there are those who turn the world upside down. Which do you want to be?

They were accused of turning the world upside down just because they had a story to tell. They used whatever talents and gifts they had to tell it. They went wherever God called them to share it. They crossed religious, racial, social, and physical barriers to spread it. They faced persecution, imprisonment, torture, and death to deliver it.

Because He's worth it.

If you have become a follower of Jesus Christ, then He has already turned your world upside down. That's what God does best.

He takes the dirtiest sinners and makes them clean.

He takes the rejected and makes them accepted in Him.

He takes the lonely and gives them a family.

He takes the broken and makes them beautiful.

He takes the hurting and makes them whole.

He takes the poor and makes them rich.

He takes those lost and calls them found.

He takes their rags and gives them His righteousness.

He takes their chaos and confusion and gives them joy and peace.

That's the beauty of the Gospel. It's the divine exchange—heaven for hell, light for darkness, love for hate.

You want to know how to turn your world upside down for God? Just go share your story. Tell what Jesus has done for you.

When the woman at the well met Jesus, she had to run and tell. Look at how she changed her world:

"Many of the Samaritans from that town believed in him because of the woman's testimony . . ." (John 4:39a).

The Samaritans were half-breeds—Jews who had intermarried with other cultures, despised by the "pure" Jews. But many of them believed in Jesus because of one woman's testimony.

She certainly changed her world.

You don't have to be a pastor, missionary, or evangelist. You don't have to have a huge ministry or be on a stage, a book cover, or a record label. You don't have to get the most likes, shares, or comments.

You just need a Jesus story.

"Then Jesus said to his disciples, 'If anyone would come after me, he must deny himself and take up his cross and follow me. For whoever wants to save his life will lose it, but whoever loses his life for me will find it" (Matthew 16:24-25).

Are you willing to lay down your life to follow Jesus—to seek Him first above all else, listen for His voice, and walk in His ways?

Yes?

Then what are you waiting for? Go change your world.

CONCLUSION

As I wrap up my thoughts, I want to go back to the title of this book. It's certainly nothing dramatic or even very original, but it is what the Lord gave me.

And it's the whole point.

Seek.

Greek word: zēteō

Meaning: "to look for, seek out, to try to obtain, desire to possess, strive for"[10]

Him.

Jesus Christ, Yeshua, the Son of God, Messiah, Savior, King of kings, Lord of lords, Immanuel, Prince of Peace, Bread of Life, Living Water, the Way, the Truth, and the Life

First.

Greek Word: prōton

Meaning: "first, earlier, above all"[11]

Life is busy. I get it. Most of us truly want to make a difference in the world, but life just gets in the way.

Do we want that to be our testimony?

It doesn't have to be.

I have found after many years of following Jesus that if I will just seek Him first, above all else, He will take care of the rest.

You can do this one thing.

As you seek Him first each day, He will speak.

As He speaks to you, He will lead you into His will for you.

As you follow His will for you, He will use you to change your world.

But it all starts here:

Seek Him first.

HOW TO HAVE NEW LIFE

Do you want to know how to have new life?

We were each created by God to know and worship Him. God loves you and desires a personal relationship with you.

The Bible teaches us that we are all sinners. Romans 3:23 says, "for all have sinned and fall short of the glory of God." God is holy and righteous and good. He created the world and all that is in it. But we are all born with a sinful nature because He made us with a free will—the opportunity to choose whether or not we will follow Him. Left to ourselves, we will fall short of His glory and righteousness. This sin separates us from God and leads only to death. Romans 6:23 says, "for the wages of sin is death."

Because God loves us so much, He made a way for us to know Him through His Son. "But God demonstrates his own love for us in this: while we were still sinners, Christ died for us" (Romans 5:8). God sent His only Son, Jesus, who lived a perfect life, to die on the cross for us as payment for our sin. He took the punishment on Himself so that we could be free from sin's penalty.

The rest of Romans 6:23 (above) says this: "but the gift of God is eternal life in Christ Jesus." We are sinners, and yet through Jesus and the gift of God, we can have eternal life. The truth is that we really can have a personal relationship with God through His Son, Jesus.

So, what do you do to be saved?

Romans 10:9-10 tells us "That if you confess with your mouth, 'Jesus is Lord,' and believe in your heart that God raised him from the dead, you will be saved. For it is with your heart that you believe and are justified, and it is with your mouth that you confess and are saved."

If God is speaking to your heart right now and you want to be saved, pray a prayer like this one:

Lord God,

I believe that You are God and that You created me to know You. I believe that You sent your Son to die on the cross for my sins and that He rose again and lives forever. I know that I am a sinner and I confess my sins to You now. I ask You to forgive me and cleanse me and come to live inside my heart and be the Lord of my life. I choose to follow You and live for You from this day forward.

In Jesus' name,

Amen

If you just prayed a prayer like this one, please let me know the good news. Find a Bible-believing Christian church and begin to read the Bible and talk to God every day. You've just begun your new life in Him. Congratulations! Your life will never be the same!

THE FOCUSED 15 CHALLENGE

Now that you have been challenged to seek Him first each day, you may be wondering how to make that a reality in your everyday life.

After all, groceries must be shopped, laundry folded, homework checked, meals prepared, work done, relationships built, ministry carried out. And even when we have the best of intentions, it's really hard to stay consistent with an in-depth Bible study.

In the FOCUSED 15 Challenge, I will show you how to study the Bible in just 15 minutes a day. I'm not talking about reading a daily devotional. I'm talking about getting into the Word so you can grow your faith.

In the FOCUSED 15 Challenge you will learn to

- Prepare with the right strategies
- Protect your 15 minutes
- Prioritize with the right resources
- Plan ahead for maximum impact
- Pursue Jesus with all your heart

And best of all, it's FREE!

So, don't let the enemy keep you busy, distracted, and unfulfilled. God has so much more for you than that. When you open your Bible, meditate on its truth, and apply it to your life, the Holy Spirit will work with you to grow your relationship with Him.

Visit https://www.subscribepage.com/focused15challengecampaign to sign up now!

CHECK OUT OUR OTHER
BOOKS ON AMAZON

Bible Studies & Devotionals

INSIDE OU
and
Upside Dow
How Intimacy with Jesus
Changes Everything
A Study on Discipleship

Seeki
TRUT
365 Days in the Wisdom an
Poetic Books of the Bible

LIVING
Faith
A Study of Hebrews 11

Just Like
US
Wisdom from the Women
of the Bible

Jennifer Hayes Ya...   Jennifer Hayes Yates   Jennifer Hayes Yates   nnifer Hayes Yates

Get grounded and grow
your faith.

**DOWNLOAD OR
ORDER NOW**

jenniferhyates.com

https://www.amazon.com/stores/
Jennifer-Hayes-Yates/author/B07581GZ84

ACKNOWLEDGMENTS

I would like to thank those in my life whose prayers, encouragement, and participation have brought this project to fruition.

Kenneth, your love and support amaze me more every day. You never fail to be my biggest supporter and encourager. Thank you for giving me the space to write, the boost to my confidence, and the love that never lets me go.

Josiah, thank you for your prayers, wisdom, and editing skills. I love you so much.

Bethany, thank you for always knowing what to say when I'm having a bad day. You are my heart.

Mema, I couldn't do any ministry without your prayers and presence in my life. And editing.

To my Bible study group, you are my inspiration. I write because of my passion for you to run hard after Jesus. Disciples making disciple-making disciples. I love you guys!

To my church family, thank you for your love, grace, and smiling faces. You encourage me to keep going.

Thank you to my accountability partner, Kristen Tiber. Your encouragement means more than you know.

Genesis and Vance, thank you for all the photo shoots, book tables, and my website. Your help has been invaluable.

Thanks to Chandler Bolt, Sean Sumner, and all those in the Self-Publishing School.

Most of all, thank you Jesus for lifting me out of the slimy pit and giving me a firm place to stand. I love You.

ABOUT THE AUTHOR

Jennifer Hayes Yates is a wife, mama, writer, and speaker with an empty nest and a Southern accent. Having taught in Christian education for twenty-two years, she has a passion for communicating God's truth and inspiring busy women to grow their faith one quiet moment with Jesus at a time.

Jennifer is now a blogger, best-selling author, and passionate speaker. Lover of all things Jesus, books, and coffee, she can be found in quiet corners or busy spaces, sipping lattes, studying commentaries, and chatting up strangers.

But she's still just a small-town girl hoping to glorify God in all she writes and make a few disciples along the way.

You can follow Jennifer on Facebook, Instagram, and at Jenniferhyates.com.

Thank you for purchasing this book!

I would love to get your feedback. If you were blessed by reading Seek Him First, please consider leaving a review on Amazon (www.amazon.com/Seek-Him-First-Change-World-ebook/dp/B078LJRZWR/). Thanks so much!

Jen

SELF-PUBLISHING
SCHOOL

NOW IT'S YOUR TURN

**Discover the EXACT 3-step blueprint you need
to become a bestselling author in 3 months.**

Self-Publishing School helped me, and now
I want them to help you with this FREE WEBINAR!

Even if you're busy, bad at writing, or don't know where to start,
you CAN write a bestseller and build your best life.

With tools and experience across a variety of niches
and professions, Self-Publishing School is the only
resource you need to take your book to the finish line!

DON'T WAIT

Watch this FREE WEBINAR now,
and Say "YES" to becoming a bestseller:

[https://xe172.isrefer.com/go/sps4fta-vts/bookbrosinc4485]

ENDNOTES

[1] Rick Warren, *Bible Study Methods* (Grand Rapids, MI: Zondervan, 2006).

[2] John R. Kohlenberger III, *The NIV Exhaustive Bible Concordance*, Third Edition (Grand Rapids, MI: Zondervan, 2015).

[3] George Knight and James Edwards, *Compact Bible Handbook*, Nelson's Compact Series (Nashville, TN: Thomas Nelson, Inc., 2004).

[4] Beth Moore, *David: Seeking a Heart Like His*, (Nashville, TN: Lifeway Press, 2010).

[5] Kohlenberger, *The NIV Exhaustive Bible Concordance*, 1568.

[6] Ibid, 1558.

[7] Ibid, 1576.

[8] Ibid, 1510.

[9] Darrell Evans, *The Best of Darrel Evans* (Vertical Music, 2002).

[10] Kohlenberger, *The NIV Exhaustive Bible Concordance, 1532.*

[11] Ibid, 1562.

Made in the USA
Las Vegas, NV
07 December 2023

82299938R00075